HMH |  into Science™

Grade 2

# My book

_____

## Look at the cover.

I notice _____

_____

I wonder _____

_____

## I am a scientist.

I observe.

I question.

I measure.

I record.

## What does your robot look like?

## Science makes me feel ...

## I like science because ...

_____

_____

_____

_____

# Consulting Authors

**Michael A. DiSpezio**
*Global Educator*
North Falmouth, Massachusetts

**Marjorie Frank**
*Science Writer and Content-Area
  Reading Specialist*
Brooklyn, New York

**Michael R. Heithaus, PhD**
*Dean, College of Arts, Sciences &
  Education Professor, Department
  of Biological Sciences*
Florida International University
Miami, Florida

**Peter McLaren**
*Executive Director of Next Gen
  Education, LLC*
Providence, Rhode Island

**Bernadine Okoro
Social Emotional
Learning Consultant**
*STEM Learning Advocate & Consultant*
Washington, DC

**Cary Sneider, PhD**
*Associate Research Professor*
Portland State University
Portland, Oregon

# Program Advisors

**Paul D. Asimow, PhD**
*Eleanor and John R. McMillan Professor of Geology
  and Geochemistry*
California Institute of Technology
Pasadena, California

**Eileen Cashman, PhD**
*Professor of Environmental Resources Engineering*
Humboldt State University
Arcata, California

**Mark B. Moldwin, PhD**
*Professor of Climate and Space Sciences and
  Engineering*
University of Michigan
Ann Arbor, Michigan

**Kelly Y. Neiles, PhD**
*Associate Professor
  of Chemistry*
St. Mary's College of Maryland
St. Mary's City, Maryland

**Sten Odenwald, PhD**
*Astronomer*
NASA Goddard Spaceflight
  Center
Greenbelt, Maryland

**Bruce W. Schafer**
*Director of K-12 STEM Collaborations, Retired*
Oregon University System
Portland, Oregon

**Barry A. Van Deman**
*President and CEO*
Museum of Life and Science
Durham, North Carolina

**Kim Withers, PhD**
*Assistant Professor*
Texas A&M
  University-Corpus Christi
Corpus Christi, Texas

## Classroom Reviewers

**Julie Ahern**
Andrew Cooke Magnet School
Waukegan, Illinois

**Amy Berke**
South Park Elementary School
Rapid City, South Dakota

**Pamela Bluestein**
Sycamore Canyon School
Newbury Park, California

**Kelly Brotz**
Cooper Elementary School
Sheboygan, Wisconsin

**Andrea Brown**
HLPUSD Science and STEAM
   TOSA, Retired
Hacienda Heights, California

**Marsha Campbell**
Murray Elementary School
Hobbs, New Mexico

**Leslie C. Antosy-Flores**
Star View Elementary School
Midway City, California

**Theresa Gailliout**
James R. Ludlow Elementary
   School
Philadelphia, Pennsylvania

**Emily Giles**
*Assistant Principal*
White's Tower Elementary School
Independence, KY

**Robert Gray**
Essex Elementary School
Baltimore, Maryland

**Stephanie Greene**
*Science Department Chair*
Sun Valley Magnet School
Sun Valley, California

**Roya Hosseini**
Junction Avenue K–8 School
Livermore, California

**Rana Mujtaba Khan**
Will Rogers High School
Van Nuys, California

**George Kwong**
Schafer Park Elementary School
Hayward, California

**Kristin Kyde**
Templeton Middle School
Sussex, Wisconsin

**Marie LaCross**
Sulphur Springs United
   School District
Santa Clarita, California

**Bonnie Lock**
La Center Elementary School
La Center, Washington

**Imelda Madrid**
*Assistant Principal*
Montague Charter Academy for
   the Arts and Sciences
Pacoima, CA

**Susana Martinez O'Brien**
Diocese of San Diego
San Diego, California

**Kara Miller**
Ridgeview Elementary School
Beckley, West Virginia

**Mercy D. Momary**
Local District Northwest
Los Angeles, California

**Dena Morosin**
Shasta Elementary School
Klamath Falls, Oregon

**Craig Moss**
Mt. Gleason Middle School
Sunland, California

**Joanna O'Brien**
Palmyra Elementary School
Palmyra, Missouri

**Wendy Savaske**
*Education Consultant*
Wisconsin Department of
   Public Instruction

**Isabel Souto**
Schafer Park Elementary School
Hayward, California

**Michelle Sullivan**
Balboa Elementary School
San Diego, California

**April Thompson**
Roll Hill School
Cincinnati, Ohio

**Tina Topoleski**
*District Science Supervisor*
Jackson School District
Jackson, New Jersey

**Terri Trebilcock**
Fairmount Elementary School
Golden, Colorado

**Emily R.C.G. Williams**
South Pasadena Middle School
South Pasadena, California

These are some smart people!

COOL!

# Unit 3 Earth's Surface

© Houghton Mifflin Harcourt Publishing Company • Image Credits: ©Aeriea/Shutterstock

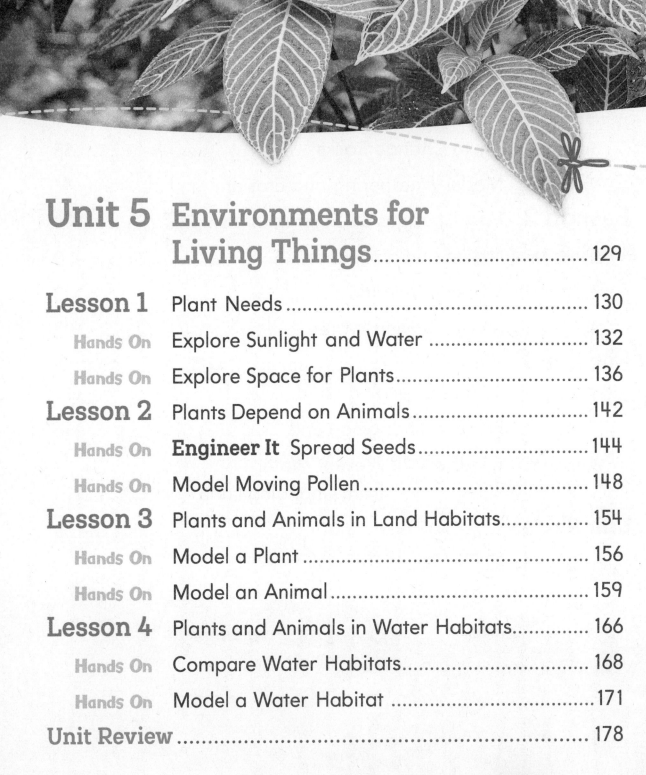

# Unit 5 Environments for Living Things

© Houghton Mifflin Harcourt Publishing Company • Image Credits: ©Fomin Serhii/Shutterstock

# Designing Solutions

A ferry boat and a bridge help people cross water. They are both solutions to the same problem. A **solution** is something that fixes a problem.

An **engineer** uses math and science to solve problems, such as how to cross water. Engineers use a design process to help them find good solutions to problems.

You can use a design process, too! A **design process** is a set of steps that helps you find a solution.

## Explore

Find out more about the
problem. You can find
better solutions when
you know more about a
problem.

Explore the problem in
the picture. Tell how you
can get more information
about the problem.

## Make

Think of as many solutions as you can. Then
make a plan for how each solution might
solve the problem. You may make and test
many solutions.

What solution do you think will best solve
the problem in the picture?

Test a solution to see how well it works. If it does not work, choose another solution or change the solution. Test again to see how the changed solution worked.

More than one solution may solve a problem. Compare the solutions to choose which works better.

Observe the solutions. Fill in the chart.

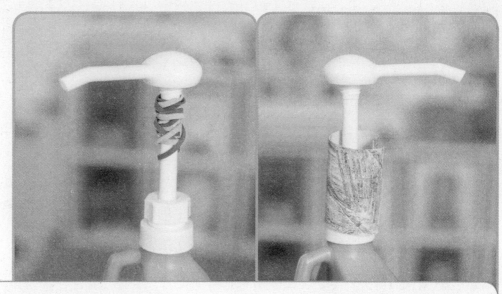

|  | Solution 1 | Solution 2 |
|---|---|---|
| Good features |  |  |
| Flawed features |  |  |

# Make It Better

Make a change you think will make a good solution better. Test the changed solution.

Why might you change and test a solution many times?

_____

_____

_____

Sometimes you might go back to the Explore or Make steps if you get new information. You can repeat any steps when you need to.

# Claims, Evidence, and Reasoning

## Make a Claim

A **claim** is a statement you think is true.

You can make a claim about what you observe.

> Some solid things sink.

A claim can be made before you investigate.

> Both the lemon and lime will sink.

A claim can be made after you investigate.

> Lemons float in water, and limes sink.

# Use Evidence and Reasoning

**Evidence** is information that shows whether or not your claim is true.

Data can be used as evidence. Evidence can come from things you observe or read.

My claim was wrong. A lemon will float, and a lime will sink.

**Reasoning** tells how or why the evidence supports the claim. You can tell why your claim is true or not. You can tell how you know.

My evidence showed that the lemon floats and the lime sinks. This proves my first claim was not true and my second claim was true.

# Safety in Science

Doing science is fun. But a science lab can be dangerous. Know the safety rules and listen to your teacher.

- ⊘ Do not eat or drink anything.
- ⊘ Do not touch sharp things.
- ✔ Wash your hands.
- ✔ Wear goggles to keep your eyes safe.
- ✔ Be neat and clean up spills.
- ✔ Tell your teacher if something breaks.
- ✔ Show good behavior.

Circle the pictures where a safety rule is being followed. Place an X on the pictures where a safety rule is not being followed.

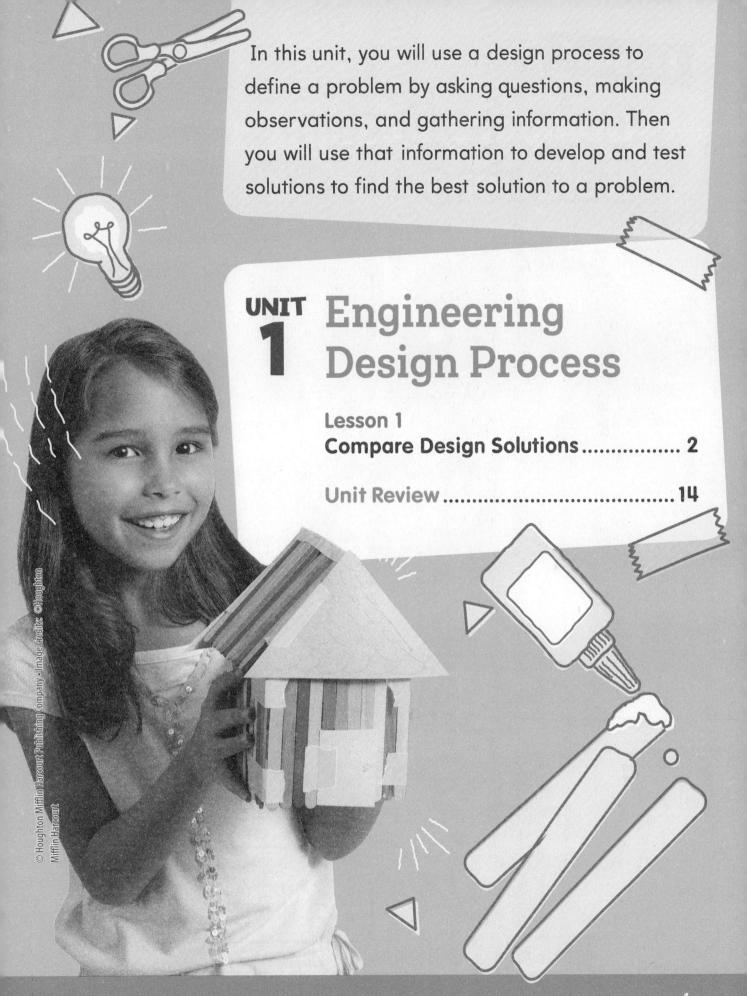

In this unit, you will use a design process to define a problem by asking questions, making observations, and gathering information. Then you will use that information to develop and test solutions to find the best solution to a problem.

# UNIT 1 Engineering Design Process

# Compare Design Solutions

Heavy!

What do you notice about the problem of moving the box?

What do you wonder about the problem of moving the box?

## Can You Explain It?

How can we use a design process to help Emma's dad solve his problem?

_____

_____

_____

_____

# Engineer It
## Design a Ramp

This ramp solves a problem. Use a design process to explore a problem. Then make and test a model of a solution. A **model** shows what an object looks like or how it works.

Ask a question about how a design process can help you solve a problem.

## Materials Checklist

☐ a toy truck     ☐ a small block

☐ construction paper

## Explore

**Step 1**

Talk with a partner about the problem you are solving. Think about how to get more information if needed.

_____

_____

_____

## Make

**Step 2**

How you can use the materials to solve the problem? Draw or write one idea.

## Step 3

Make a model that you can test to find out how well your solution works. Record what you observe.

 Engineers do not expect to make the best solution the first time. Talk with a partner about what you will do if your first solution does not work well.

## Step 4

Compare your solution with another group. Write about what you find out.

_____

_____

_____

Make a **claim** about how a design process helps you solve a problem.

_____

_____

What is your **evidence**? Talk with a partner about your **reasoning**.

## Making Sense ■ □

I explored _____

_____

_____

How does this help me explain how Emma's dad can use a design process to help him solve his problem?

_____

_____

_____

# Engineer It
### Compare Features

The shape and material of a ramp can change how it works. Compare the two ramps shown. What is the same about them? What is different?

Ask a question about what makes a good ramp.

_____

_____

_____

## Materials Checklist

☐ a toy truck   ☐ a small block   ☐ craft materials

## Make It Better

**Step 1**

Observe the materials. How can you use them to improve your solution from the last activity? Talk with a partner.

**Step 2**

Make a plan to test two other materials.

**Step 3**

Follow your plan. Test each model. Compare the solutions.

| | Good features | Flawed features |
|---|---|---|
| Solution 1 | | |
| Solution 2 | | |

Make a **claim** about how comparing features of solutions can help you find a better solution.

_____

_____


What is your **evidence**? Talk with a partner about your **reasoning**.


## Making Sense

I explored _____

_____

_____


How does this help me explain how Emma's dad can use a design process to help him solve his problem?

_____

_____

# Lesson Check

## Can You Explain It?

How can we use a design process to help Emma's dad solve his problem? Be sure to describe how steps in a design process can help in finding a better solution.

_____

_____

_____

_____

# Self Check

1. Which would you do first when using a design process to solve a problem?

    Ⓐ Explore the problem.

    Ⓑ Make a solution.

    Ⓒ Make the solution better.

2. Describe how the girl is using the drawing as part of a design process.

_____

_____

_____

_____

**3.** Which of the following is true? Choose all correct answers.

(A) Only one solution can solve a problem.

(B) Multiple solutions can solve a problem.

(C) Some solutions are better than other solutions.

**4.** Manuel tests model cars he built for a race. The table shows the data. Explain which car Manuel should choose. Use evidence and reasoning to support your claim.

|  | **Good features** | **Flawed features** |
|---|---|---|
| Car 1 | looks nice | slow |
| Car 2 | fastest | expensive |
| Car 3 | medium speed | does not look nice |

_____

_____

_____

_____

# Unit Review

1. The problem with this grocery bag is that its bottom is too _____.

   (A) strong

   (B) weak

   (C) brown

2. Kayla tests model cars she built for a race. What helps her decide which car to choose for the race?

   (A) color

   (B) data

   (C) feelings

3. Arum sees a boy with his pant leg caught on a bike chain. How can she help him solve this problem?

   _____

   _____

   _____

**4.** Explain why it is important to explore a problem before you begin finding a solution.

_____

_____

_____

**5.** Which might you do next if a possible solution does not solve the problem? Choose all correct answers.

(A) Make and test new solutions.

(B) Test the same solution until it works.

(C) Change the solution and test again.

**6.** These children are designing a parachute. What part of a design process are they doing?

(A) planning

(B) building

(C) testing

**7.** Yolanda wants to keep the sun off her face. Explain which hat she should choose and why.

straw hat

knit hat

narrow brim hat

_____

_____

_____

_____

**8.** Explain two ways a model can be used in a design process.

_____

_____

_____

_____

In Unit 1, you used a design process to find and build the best solution to a problem. In Unit 2, you will analyze information you gather from tests on properties of materials to choose the best materials to solve a problem.

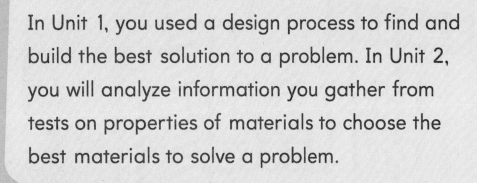

# UNIT 2 Matter

# Lesson 1
# Properties of Matter

Game on!

What do you notice about the different balls?

What do you wonder about the different balls?

## Can You Explain It?

Why do we use a basketball in one sport
and a baseball in a different sport?

_____

_____

_____

_____

# Sort Objects

## All these balls are matter.

**Matter** is anything that takes up space.
You can describe matter by its properties.
A **property** is one part of what something
is like.

Ask a question about how you can sort
objects by their properties.

_____

_____

_____

_____

## Materials Checklist

- ☐ a cotton ball
- ☐ a chenille stick
- ☐ a rubber ball
- ☐ a wooden block

*cool!*

## Step 1

Record properties you observe about the objects.

_____

_____

_____

## Step 2

Plan a way to sort the objects by their properties. Follow your plan.

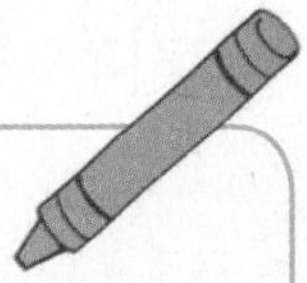

Explain your results. Look for patterns.

Make a **claim** about how you can sort objects by their properties.

_____

_____

What is your **evidence**? Talk with a partner about your **reasoning**.

## Making Sense

I explored _____

_____

_____

How does this help me explain why we use a basketball in one sport and a baseball in a different sport?

_____

_____

# Engineer It
## Explore Properties

Think about the properties of a pillow. Should a pillow be soft? Should it be firm? Pillows are filled with different materials, making them good for resting your head or even pillow fights.

Ask a question about what properties make the best filling for a pillow.

_____

_____

_____

_____

## Materials Checklist

☐ a pillowcase    ☐ cotton    ☐ foam    ☐ feathers

## Explore
### Step 1

Explore the problem.

## Make
### Step 2

Plan two ways to solve the problem. Build your solutions.

CLOUDS;-)

| Plan 1 | Plan 2 |
|---|---|
|  |  |

 Why is it important to have a plan before you start building your solutions?

## Make
**Step 3**

Test your solutions. Record and compare the results of each filling you tested.

_____

_____

_____

## Make It Better
**Step 4**

Choose one solution. Make it better. You can try different materials.

**Step 5**

Share your solution with your classmates. Compare solutions.

Make a **claim** about what properties make the best filling for a pillow.

_____

_____

_____

What is your **evidence**? Talk with a partner about your **reasoning**.

## Making Sense

I explored _____

_____

_____

How does this help me explain why we use a basketball in one sport and a baseball in a different sport?

_____

_____

# Lesson Check

## Can You Explain It?

Why do we use a basketball in one sport and a baseball in a different sport? Be sure to describe how properties are connected to the way things work.

_____

_____

_____

_____

_____

# Self Check

1. Dax sorts these materials by using a property. Look for a pattern. Which property does he sort by?

   Ⓐ color

   Ⓑ shape

   Ⓒ texture

2. Michael's feet slip when he pedals his bike. He tests three materials to help stop his feet from slipping off the pedals.

| Michael's Test | |
|---|---|
| **Material** | **Number of slips** |
| aluminum foil | 7 |
| cardboard | 5 |
| sandpaper | 2 |

Look closely at the data for patterns. Which material works best?

   Ⓐ aluminum foil

   Ⓑ cardboard

   Ⓒ sandpaper

**3.** Mila wants to use clay to design a shape that will roll across the floor. What kind of properties should the shape have?

_____

_____

_____

_____

**4.** Mila's first shape is a cube. It does not roll well. What could she do to her shape to help it roll better?

_____

_____

_____

_____

# Objects Can Be Put Together

Building is fun!

© Houghton Mifflin Harcourt Publishing Company • Image Credits: (t) ©Houghton Mifflin Harcourt; (b) ©Houghton Mifflin Harcourt

What do you notice about the toy truck and toy boat?

What do you wonder about the toy truck and toy boat?

## Can You Explain It?

How can a toy truck change shape to become a toy boat?

_____

_____

_____

_____

# Explore What Objects Are Made Of

You can make new objects from smaller pieces. This house has windows, a door, and a roof. It uses materials like glass, wood, and stone. Each piece helps support the building in different ways.

Ask a question about how each piece is used.

_____

_____

## Materials Checklist

NEAT!

☐ pictures of buildings made of different materials

## Step 1

Observe the buildings in the pictures.
Choose one building. Tell about its parts.
What is each part made of?

_____

_____

_____

## Step 2

Design your own building. Label the parts.
Write about what the parts are made of.

Compare your buildings with others.

Make a **claim** about why buildings are made of different pieces.

_____

_____

What is your **evidence**? Talk with a partner about your **reasoning**.

## Making Sense

I explored _____

_____

_____

How does this help me explain how a toy truck can become a toy boat?

_____

_____

_____

# Build Objects From Smaller Pieces

Think about the pieces that make up these two toy buildings. Each building uses the same set of pieces but in a different way. Observe how one building can become another building.

Ask a question about how objects can be taken apart and put together in new ways.

_____

_____

_____

## Materials Checklist

☐ non-hardening clay    ☐ toothpicks    ☐ paper clips

☐ erasers    ☐ a plastic zip bag

## Step 1

Make a plan to find out how many objects you can build from the same set of pieces.

## Step 2

Follow your plan. Draw to record each object you build.

 What can you do if you struggle to come up with different objects to build?

## Step 3

How are the objects you build alike? How are they different?

| Alike | Different |
|---|---|
| | |

## Step 4

Compare your objects with objects that your classmates make.

Make a **claim** about how you can build objects from the same set of pieces.

_____

_____

_____

What is your **evidence**? Talk with a partner about your **reasoning**.

## Making Sense

I explored _____

_____

_____

How does this help me explain how a toy truck can become a toy boat?

_____

_____

_____

# Lesson Check

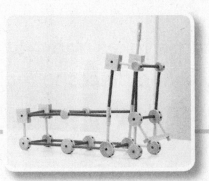

## Can You Explain It?

How can a toy truck change shape to become a toy boat? Be sure to explain how parts of objects are connected to how they are put together.

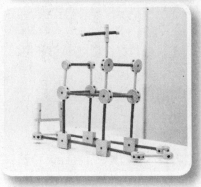

_____

_____

_____

_____

_____

# Self Check

1. Michelle takes apart an old toy. She reuses the pieces to make a new one. How could the toy have changed? Choose all correct answers.

   Ⓐ It changed color.

   Ⓑ It changed shape.

   Ⓒ It changed size.

2. You can make new objects from smaller pieces. How would you use the bricks, the door, and the window to make a new object?

_____

_____

_____

**3.** How can you build this object from smaller pieces? Number the pictures 1, 2, and 3 to show the correct order.

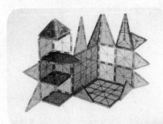  

_____ _____ _____

**4.** Zachary builds a house with blocks. How can he use those blocks to build a new object?

_____

_____

_____

# Lesson 3
# Matter Can Change

Turn up the heat!

What do you notice about the icicles and
the bread?

What do you wonder about the icicles and
the bread?

## Can You Explain It?

How do icicles and bread change in
different ways?

_____

_____

_____

_____

# Explore Cooling

SPLASH!

BRRR!

Cooling can cause matter to **freeze**, or change from a liquid to a solid. Changes to matter that can be undone are **reversible**. Changes that cannot be undone are **irreversible**.

Ask a question about how cooling may change matter.

## Materials Checklist

☐ an ice cube     ☐ a cup of water

☐ a wooden block     ☐ a flower

COOL!

## Step 1

Observe the items. What do you think will happen to them when they are put in a freezer?

_____

_____

_____

## Step 2

Put all the items in a freezer overnight. Take them out the next day.

## Step 3

What effect does freezing have on each item?

| | |
|---|---|
| ice cube | |
| water | |
| block | |
| flower | |

## Step 4

Can the flower and the water go back to what they were? How could you find out? Talk with a partner about whether the changes are reversible or irreversible.

 Why is it important to follow the steps of your investigation in order?

© Houghton Mifflin Harcourt Publishing Company • Image Credits: (tr) ©Houghton Mifflin Harcourt

Make a **claim** about how cooling affects different objects.

_____

_____

_____

What is your **evidence**? Talk with a partner about your **reasoning**.

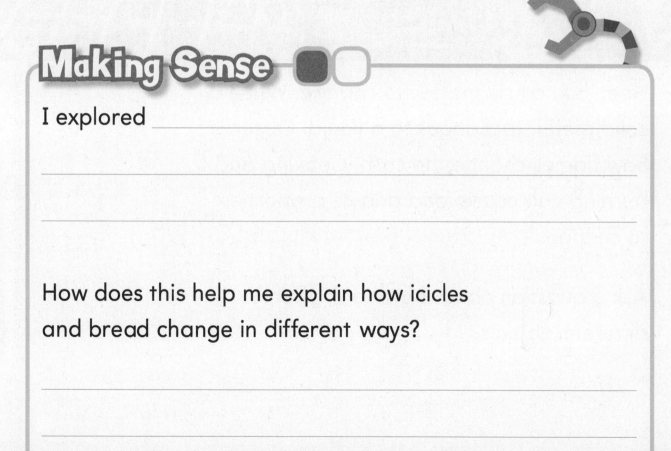

**Making Sense**

I explored _____

_____

_____

How does this help me explain how icicles and bread change in different ways?

_____

_____

© Houghton Mifflin Harcourt Publishing Company

# Explore Heating

Heat can cause matter to change. When a solid **melts**, it changes to a liquid. Observe how flames change the corn. Cooking and burning can cause food and its properties to change.

Ask a question about how heat affects different objects.

## Materials Checklist

- [ ] an ice pop
- [ ] a brown bag
- [ ] popcorn kernels
- [ ] paper plates

LOOK!

## Step 1

Observe the items and their properties. Talk with a partner.

## Step 2

Put the kernels in the bag. Keep the ice pop on a plate. Your teacher will put each item in the microwave.

## Step 3

Record your observations. What effect does heating have on the ice pop and the kernels?

_____

_____

_____

Can the popcorn and the ice pop go back to what they were? How could you find out? Talk with a partner about whether each change is reversible or irreversible.

Make a **claim** about how heat affects different objects.

_____

_____

What is your **evidence**? Talk with a partner about your **reasoning**.

## Making Sense ■ ■

I explored _____

_____

How does this help me explain how icicles and bread change in different ways?

_____

_____

# Lesson Check

## Can You Explain It?

How do icicles and bread change in different ways? Be sure to explain how heating and cooling are connected to reversible and irreversible changes.

_____

_____

_____

_____

_____

# Self Check

1. Look at the snow and the wax. What pattern do you see?

Ⓐ The materials change from liquid to solid.

Ⓑ The materials change from solid to liquid.

Ⓒ The materials change to ashes.

2. Elizabeth places juice in a freezer. The next day she observes that the juice is frozen. What evidence does Elizabeth have to make the argument that the juice froze?

Ⓐ The juice changes from liquid to solid.

Ⓑ The juice changes from solid to liquid.

Ⓒ The juice changes color only.

**3.** What evidence do the pictures give to show that this change is reversible?

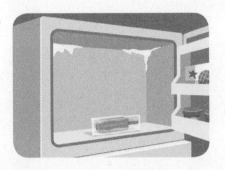 

_____

_____

_____

_____

**4.** Which changes are reversible? Which changes are irreversible? Write **reversible** or **irreversible** to identify each change.

| Cause | Effect | Change |
|---|---|---|
| Fire burns wood. | Wood turns to ash. | |
| Freezer freezes lemonade. | Lemonade turns solid. | |
| Heat cooks popcorn kernels. | Kernels turn white and fluffy. | |

# Unit Review

1. What causes water to freeze?

   Ⓐ Heat is added to water.

   Ⓑ Water is cooked too much.

   Ⓒ Heat is taken away from water.

2. What pattern occurs when matter is melted?

   Ⓐ It changes from a liquid to ashes.

   Ⓑ It changes from a solid to a liquid.

   Ⓒ It changes from a liquid to a solid.

3. Look at the wax and the muffin batter. Which statements are true? Choose all correct answers.

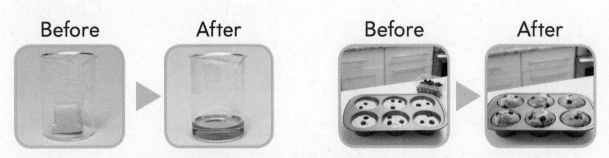

Before          After                Before          After

   Ⓐ Heat causes the wax to melt.

   Ⓑ Heat causes the muffin batter to cook.

   Ⓒ Heat causes the wax and muffin batter to burn and turn to ashes.

**4.** Describe a way you could sort these objects by their properties.

_____

_____

_____

**5.** Emma wants to find out whether feathers or foam make a better pillow filler. What could she do?

Ⓐ She could test only the feathers.

Ⓑ She could test only the foam.

Ⓒ She could test both the feathers and the foam.

**6.** Which change caused by heating is irreversible?

Ⓐ a crayon melting

Ⓑ butter melting

Ⓒ paper burning

**7.** How can you build the cube from smaller pieces? Number the pictures 1, 2, and 3 to show the correct order.

 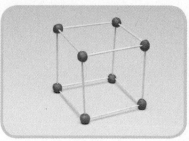 

_____

**8.** What caused the change? Is it reversible or irreversible? Make a claim about it. Use evidence to support your answer.

_____

_____

_____

_____

In Unit 2, you explored properties of matter and how it can change. In this unit, you will observe how these changes cause patterns in the water and land. You will develop maps that can model these patterns on Earth's surface.

# UNIT 3 Earth's Surface

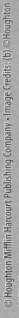

# Lesson 1
# Water on Earth

Go with the flow.

What do you notice about the river?

What do you wonder about the river?

## Can You Explain It?

What causes the river to look different during different times of the year?

# Hands On!

# Observe Water All Around

Water is all around us. In fact, most of Earth is covered in water! Think about where you have seen water on Earth. What bodies of water can you see in the picture?

Ask a question about where water is found on Earth.

_____

_____

## Materials Checklist

☐ nonfiction books  ☐ a computer  ☐ crayons or markers

### Step 1

In your group, look up information about the body of water your teacher gave you.

### Step 2

Draw a picture of the body of water you looked up. Label the drawing.

### Step 3

Compare your drawing with others' drawings.

| alike | different |
|-------|-----------|
|       |           |
|       |           |

## Step 4

Analyze your results. Look for patterns.

Make a **claim** about bodies of water on Earth.

_____

_____

What is your **evidence**? Talk with a
partner about your **reasoning**.

## Making Sense

I explored _____

_____

_____

How does this help me explain what causes
a river to look different during different
times of the year?

_____

# Observe Temperature Changes to Water

Glaciers are slow moving sheets of ice. They may be very large and take a long time to form. Sometimes parts of a glacier can melt even in cold areas where glaciers are found.

Ask a question about how water changes with temperature.

_____

_____

_____

## Materials Checklist

☐ modeling clay  ☐ a cup of water

☐ refrigerator  ☐ freezer

### Step 1

Make a plan to find out how temperature affects a body of water. Think about how you can use a model of a body of water in your plan. How could a refrigerator or freezer help you?

 How do I decide what I do first, next, and last?

## Step 2

Follow your plan. Record how the temperature changes affect the water in your model.

| before | after |
| --- | --- |
|  |  |

## Step 3

Compare your observations with your classmates. What patterns do you observe?

_____

_____

_____

## Step 4

What do you think can happen to some bodies of water during winter? Discuss with your class.

Make a **claim** about how temperature may affect a body of water.

_____

_____

_____

What is your **evidence**? Talk with a partner about your **reasoning**.

# Making Sense ▢▢

I explored _____

_____

_____

How does this help me explain why a river may look different during different times of the year?

_____

_____

# Lesson Check

## Can You Explain It?

What causes the river to look different during different times of the year?

_____

_____

_____

# Self Check

1. Which picture shows frozen water? Circle the correct choice.

2. What is the same about these two bodies of water? What is different? Explain.

_____

_____

_____

_____

**3.** The children see a body of flowing water that has land on both sides. What body of water do they see?

   Ⓐ lake

   Ⓑ pond

   Ⓒ river

**4.** Makayla is making a model of an ocean for her science class. What patterns do oceans have that her model should show?

_____

_____

_____

Lesson 2

# Landforms on Earth

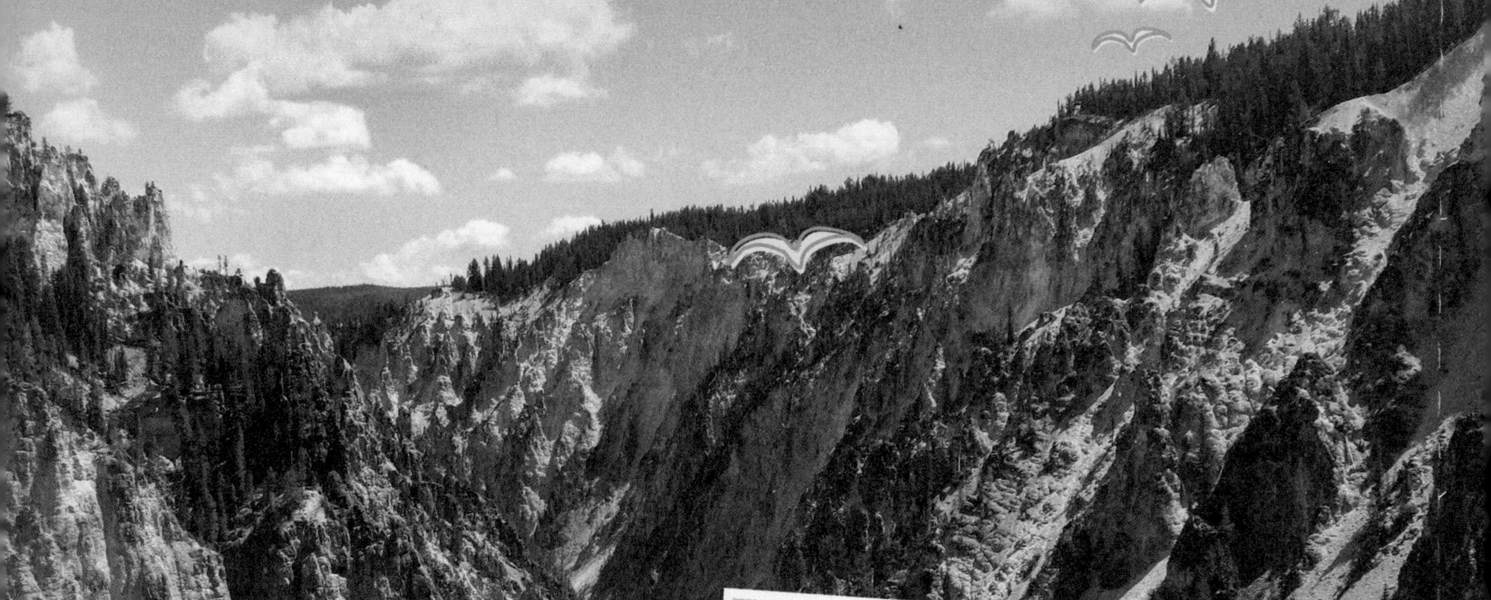

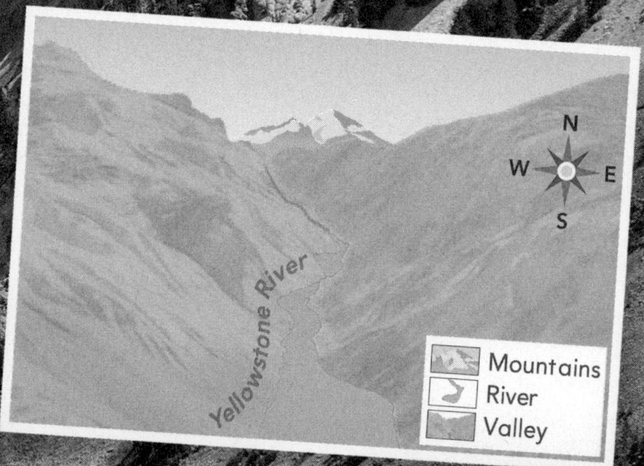
N
W
E
S
Yellowstone River
Mountains
River
Valley

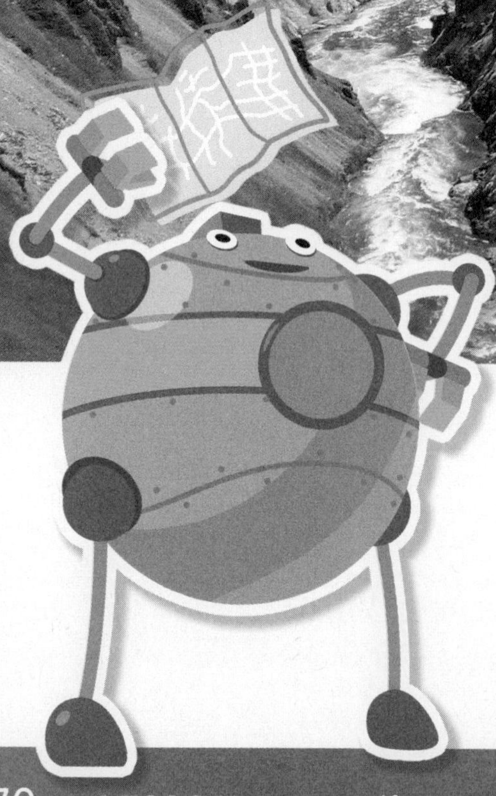

Map it!

What do you notice about the landforms
and the body of water?

What do you wonder about the landforms
and the body of water?

## Can You Explain It?

How do people show patterns of land and
water on a map?

# Model Landforms

Mountains, like the ones in the picture, are a type of landform. A **landform** is a natural feature found on Earth's surface. Other landforms include hills, valleys, and canyons.

Ask a question about landforms and how you can model them.

_____

_____

## Materials Checklist

☐ an aluminum pan   ☐ a spray bottle with water

☐ gloves   ☐ sand   ☐ markers   ☐ safety goggles

### Step 1

Look online or in books to obtain information on hills, mountains, valleys, and canyons. Discuss what you find out with your classmates.

### Step 2

Use the spray bottle to make the sand damp. Mix the sand and water together.

### Step 3

Use the damp sand to make models of two different landforms. Draw your models.

**Step 4**

Compare your drawings and models with a classmate's work. Identify any patterns you observe.

Make a **claim** about how making models helps you better understand landforms.

_____

_____

What is your **evidence**? Talk with a partner about your **reasoning**.

## Making Sense ■ ▢

I explored _____

_____

_____

How does this help explain how patterns of land can be shown on a map?

_____

_____

© Houghton Mifflin Harcourt Publishing Company

# Hands On!

# Mapping Landforms and Bodies of Water

North
West ◄—○—► East
South

**Key**
🔺 mountains
🔻 valley
⛰ hills
〰 river
🌊 lake

A map is a drawing or model of a place. It shows where things are located. It can show the shapes and kinds of land and water. A **map key** shows what the map colors and symbols mean. A **compass rose** shows the directions north, south, east, and west.

Ask a question about how landforms and bodies of water can be shown on a map.

© Houghton Mifflin Harcourt Publishing Company

## Materials Checklist

☐ maps  ☐ markers or crayons

HOW?

### Step 1

Look at different maps. What do you notice about them?

_____

_____

_____

### Step 2

Make a plan for a map of a real or made-up place. Choose at least two landforms and two bodies of water to show. Decide on a map title, or what to name your map. Include a map key and a compass rose.

Write your plan for your map.

_____

_____

_____

## Step 3

Draw your map.

What can you do if you have trouble drawing your map?

## Step 4

Compare maps with your classmates. What did you find out about making and reading maps? What patterns did you observe?

_____

_____

_____

Make a **claim** about how landforms and bodies of water can be shown on a map.

_____

_____

_____

What is your **evidence**? Talk with a partner about your **reasoning**.

## Making Sense ▢ ▢

I explored _____

_____

_____

How does this help explain how patterns of land and water are shown on a map?

_____

_____

© Houghton Mifflin Harcourt Publishing Company

# Lesson Check

## Can You Explain It?

How do people show patterns of land and water on a map?

_____

_____

_____

_____

# Self Check

1. Match each picture with the name of the correct landform.

canyon

hill

mountain

2. Explain why a map needs a map key and a compass rose.

_____

_____

_____

**3.** Which of the following patterns is shown on the map? Choose all correct answers.

Ⓐ Rivers flow through canyons.

Ⓑ Mountains are bigger than hills.

Ⓒ Bodies of water are different colors.

**4.** Compare the two landforms. What is the same? What is different?

mountain

hill

_____

_____

_____

# Unit Review

1. What patterns can a map show? Choose all correct answers.

   Ⓐ shapes of land and water

   Ⓑ where things are located

   Ⓒ the time it takes to get to a place

2. Which of the following can a model show? Choose all correct answers.

   Ⓐ shapes of landforms

   Ⓑ patterns of landforms

   Ⓒ how temperature affects bodies of water

3. Which is true of oceans? Choose all correct answers.

   Ⓐ They are made up of salt water.

   Ⓑ They are made up of fresh water.

   Ⓒ They hold most of Earth's water.

**4.** Explain what might cause a body of water to freeze.

_____

_____

_____

**5.** Look at the picture of the mountain. Explain how you can use it to help you make a model of a mountain with sand.

_____

_____

_____

**6.** Describe some ways you can use a map.

_____

_____

_____

_____

**7.** Look at each body of water. Make a claim about its patterns. Cite evidence to support your claim.

ocean

river

_____

_____

_____

_____

**8.** Draw a line to match each map part with the words that describe it.

| | |
|---|---|
| compass rose | names the place the map shows |
| key | tells what map colors and symbols mean |
| title | shows directions |

© Houghton Mifflin Harcourt Publishing Company • Image Credits: (tl) ©Matthew Williams-Ellis/robertharding/Getty Images; (tr) ©tefan/Adobe Stock

In Unit 3, you observed patterns in landforms and bodies of water and made a map to model them. In this unit, you will make observations to identify evidence that patterns in landforms and bodies of water are a result of changes to Earth's surface that can happen slowly or quickly. You will also design solutions to prevent wind and water from changing the land.

# UNIT 4 Changes to Earth's Surface

# Lesson 1
# Slow Changes on Earth

This place rocks!

What do you notice about the rocks?

What do you wonder about the rocks?

## Can You Explain It?

Why do the rocks slowly change over time?

_____

_____

_____

_____

# Try to Change Rocks

Observe the hole in the rock. It has a very unusual shape. Think about whether the change happened quickly or slowly over time.

Ask a question about the change in the rock.

_____

_____

_____

## Materials Checklist

☐ a rock ☐ sandpaper ☐ safety goggles
☐ hand lens ☐ black construction paper

NEAT!

### Step 1

Use a hand lens to observe the rock. Record what you observe.

### Step 2

Can you change the shape of the rock? Use the sandpaper. Rub the rock for 5 minutes. What happens to the rock?

Rub the rock for 2 more minutes. Talk with a partner about what you observe.

Make a **claim** about how a rock changes over time.

_____

_____

What is your **evidence**? Talk with a partner about your **reasoning**.

## Making Sense

I explored _____

_____

_____

How does this help me explain why rocks may change slowly over time?

_____

_____

# Model Weathering and Erosion

**Weathering** is a process that breaks rock into smaller pieces. **Erosion** is the picking up and moving of rocks, soil, or sand from one place to another. Think about how erosion has changed this valley.

Ask a question about how weathering and erosion change Earth's surface.

_____

_____

## Materials Checklist

☐ a sugar cube     ☐ blocks     ☐ an eyedropper

☐ a foil tray     ☐ cup of water     ☐ a hand lens

## Step 1

Use a hand lens to observe the properties of the sugar cube. Share what you observe with a partner.

## Step 2

Make a plan to model weathering and erosion by using the sugar cube.

 What can I do if I struggle to come up with a plan?

**Step 3**

Follow your plan. Compare the sugar cube before and after.

| Before | After |
|---|---|
| | |

**Step 4**

Compare observations with your classmates. How does this model show how weathering and erosion slowly change Earth's surface?

_____

_____

Make a **claim** about how weathering and erosion can cause changes to Earth's surface.

_____

_____

_____

What is your **evidence**? Talk with a partner about your **reasoning**.

## Making Sense ▢▢

I explored _____

_____

_____

How does this help me explain why rocks may change slowly over time?

_____

_____

© Houghton Mifflin Harcourt Publishing Company

Name _____

# Lesson Check

## Can You Explain It?

Why do the rocks slowly change over time? Be sure to describe what causes the rocks to change.

_____

_____

_____

_____

# Self Check

1. What is the effect of wind slowly weathering and eroding a rock?

Ⓐ The rock does not change.

Ⓑ The rock gets smaller.

Ⓒ The rock gets larger.

2. How does erosion change the land? Write 1, 2, and 3 to show the correct order.

_____     _____     _____

3. Michelle is using a cube of salt to model a rock. She has a cup of water. How can she model weathering and erosion?

_____

_____

_____

_____

4. Observe the pictures of the valley. How has it changed? Explain whether you think this change happened slowly or quickly.

_____

_____

_____

_____

# Fast Changes on Earth

What's shaking?

What do you notice about the volcano
and the earthquake?

What do you wonder about the volcano and
the earthquake?

## Can You Explain It?

How do these events quickly change
Earth's surface?

_____

_____

_____

_____

# Model an Earthquake

An **earthquake** causes a sudden shaking of the ground that makes land rise and fall. It can also cause a landslide. A **landslide** is when rocks and soil slide down a slope. Observe how the road looks different after an earthquake. Think about whether this change is fast or slow.

Ask a question about how earthquakes can change Earth's surface.

## Materials Checklist

☐ graham crackers  ☐ a paper plate

### Step 1

Record what you observe about the graham crackers.

_____

_____

_____

_____

### Step 2

Make a plan to use graham crackers to model an earthquake. Follow your plan.

© Houghton Mifflin Harcourt Publishing Company • Image Credits: (tr) ©Houghton Mifflin Harcourt

Discuss your results. Talk with a partner about whether the change was fast or slow.

Make a **claim** about how an earthquake can cause fast changes to Earth's surface.

_____

_____

What is your **evidence**? Talk with a partner about your **reasoning**.

## Making Sense ■☐☐

I explored _____

_____

How does this help me explain how events cause fast changes to Earth's surface?

_____

_____

# Hands On!

# Model a Volcano

A **volcano** is an opening in Earth's surface where lava, gases, and bits of rock erupt. Ash and dust burst from the opening at the top. You can make a model to show what happens when a volcano erupts.

Ask a question about how volcanoes can change Earth's surface.

_____

_____

_____

_____

## Materials Checklist

- [ ] dish soap
- [ ] paint
- [ ] plastic cup
- [ ] safety goggles
- [ ] baking soda
- [ ] water
- [ ] vinegar
- [ ] gloves

### Step 1

Talk with a partner about how you can model a volcanic eruption.

*HMM*

Why is it important to listen when other people are talking?

### Step 2

Mix together dish soap, baking soda, paint, and water in the cup. Record what you observe.

## Step 3

Slowly pour the vinegar into the cup. Record
what you observe.

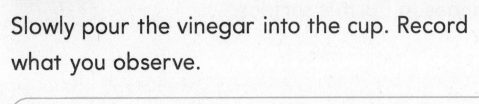

## Step 4

Discuss your observations with your partner.
How does your volcano compare to a
real volcano?

Make a **claim** about how a volcano can cause fast changes to Earth's surface.

_____

_____

_____

What is your **evidence**? Talk with a partner about your **reasoning**.

## Making Sense ▢▢▢

I explored _____

_____

_____

How does this help me explain how events cause fast changes to Earth's surface?

_____

_____

_____

# Model Moving Water

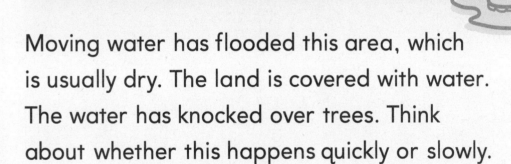

Moving water has flooded this area, which is usually dry. The land is covered with water. The water has knocked over trees. Think about whether this happens quickly or slowly.

Ask a question about how moving water can change Earth's surface.

_____

_____

_____

## Materials Checklist

- [ ] soil
- [ ] sand
- [ ] rocks
- [ ] a container
- [ ] water
- [ ] gloves
- [ ] safety goggles

NEAT

### Step 1

Make a model of land using rocks, soil, and sand. Draw your model.

### Step 2

Talk with a partner about what you think the model will look like after you add water. Will adding water be a fast change or a slow change to the land?

## Step 3

Quickly pour water onto the model. Record what you observe.

## Step 4

Compare the model before and after you added water. How does this help you understand how moving water changes an area?

_____

_____

_____

Make a **claim** about how moving water can cause fast changes to Earth's surface.

_____

_____

_____

What is your **evidence**? Talk with a partner about your **reasoning**.

## Making Sense ■ ■ ■

I explored _____

_____

_____

How does this help me explain how events cause fast changes to Earth's surface?

_____

_____

_____

# Lesson Check

## Can You Explain It?

How do these events quickly change Earth's surface? Be sure to explain what happens during each event to cause these changes.

_____

_____

_____

_____

# Self Check

1. How does moving water change Earth's surface? Write 1, 2, and 3 to show the correct order.

_____    _____    _____

2. Lava and ash have quickly covered the land. Which event caused this to happen?

Ⓐ an earthquake

Ⓑ moving water

Ⓒ a volcano erupting

**3.** Compare the pictures. How did an earthquake change Earth's surface? Explain if the change was fast or slow.

_____

_____

_____

_____

**4.** Mia's teacher shared a picture of an area with lots of trees. Then she shared a picture of the same area covered by water. How can moving water change Earth's surface?

_____

_____

_____

# Lesson 3
# Prevent Wind and Water from Changing Land

On a roll!

What do you notice about the rocks
and the technology in use?

What do you wonder about the rocks
and the technology in use?

## Can You Explain It?

How can people help prevent fast changes
to Earth's surface?

# Explore Changing Land

Crops can grow well in healthy soil. Soil can become unhealthy. This can happen quickly or slowly. For example, wind can slowly blow away healthy soil. **Windbreaks** are trees and shrubs used to block wind.

Ask a question about how wind can cause soil to become unhealthy.

_____

_____

_____

## Materials Checklist

☐ pictures of farmland

☐ pictures of windbreaks

YIKES!

## Step 1

Observe the pictures of the farmland. Talk with a partner about what causes the soil of the farmland to change.

_____

_____

## Step 2

Study the pictures of the windbreaks. With your partner, show how farmers can use trees to help stop soil from blowing away.

Compare your models to your classmates' models.

Make a **claim** about how windbreaks help farmland.

_____

_____

What is your **evidence**? Talk with a partner about your **reasoning**.

# Making Sense ▣ ▢

I explored _____

_____

_____

How does this help me explain how people help prevent fast changes to Earth's surface?

_____

_____

_____

# Engineer It
## Prevent Water from Changing Land

Rocks from landslides are not
the only things that can change
Earth's surface. Water can, too!
Moving water can quickly flood
a place and cover large areas of land.

Ask a question about how people can slow
or prevent water from changing land.

_____

_____

_____

## Materials Checklist

- ☐ sand
- ☐ soil
- ☐ rocks
- ☐ ruler
- ☐ gloves
- ☐ water
- ☐ safety goggles
- ☐ craft materials
- ☐ a container

## Explore
### Step 1

Define the problem. In small groups, talk about how water can change land.

COOL!

## Make
### Step 2

Draw a way to prevent water from changing the land. Build your model.

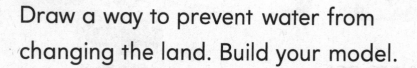

Why is it important to draw your solution before you build it?

## Step 3

Test your solution by pouring water onto the model. Observe and measure the height of its banks. Record your observations.

_____

_____

## Make It Better
### Step 4

Make your solution better. Test it again. Measure the height. Compare the two solutions.

_____

_____

## Step 5

Compare your model with other groups.

Make a **claim** about how technology can be
used to help prevent changes to land.

_____

_____

What is your **evidence**? Talk with a partner
about your **reasoning**.

## Making Sense

I explored _____

_____

_____

How does this help me explain how people
can help prevent fast changes to Earth's
surface?

_____

_____

Name _____

# Lesson Check

## Can You Explain It?

How can people help prevent fast changes to Earth's surface? Be sure to explain what causes the changes and how technology can help.

_____
_____
_____
_____
_____
_____
_____

# Self Check

1. Why would a farmer add trees and shrubs around his farm?

_____

_____

_____

_____

2. How can people prevent or slow water from changing land? Circle all correct answers.

**3.** Circle all the pictures that show changes caused by wind moving soil.

**4.** Maria has an idea for how to help her town prevent water from changing the land. How can she test her idea? What should she do if her idea does not work?

_____

_____

_____

_____

_____

# Unit Review

1. How do canyons slowly change over time?

   Ⓐ They get deeper.

   Ⓑ They get rockier.

   Ⓒ They get smaller.

2. Identify two kinds of technology that can slow or prevent moving water from changing Earth's surface. Explain which solution you think is better.

   _____

   _____

   _____

   _____

3. Does each event change Earth's surface quickly or slowly? Write **quickly** or **slowly** on the line below each picture.

4. How does the fence protect the sand dune? Choose all correct answers.

Ⓐ The fence allows animals to pass through.

Ⓑ The fence blocks some of the wind.

Ⓒ The fence keeps the sand from moving a lot.

5. Lucas has a rock and some sandpaper. He rubs the rock for 5 minutes, and nothing happens. He tries again several more times. The rock still does not change. What question could Lucas investigate further?

_____

_____

6. Which items can you use to build something that will slow or stop moving water? Circle all correct answers.

**7.** Match each event to the effect.

| | |
|---|---|
| earthquake | The ground cracks and shifts. |
| landslide | Lava and gas erupt. |
| volcano | Rocks rush down a mountain. |

**8.** Observe the farmland. Draw what could happen to the farmland if a farmer did not use windbreaks to protect the soil.

In Unit 4, you used evidence to explain that processes that cause changes to Earth's surface can happen quickly or slowly. In this unit, you will plan and carry out investigations to describe diversity of plant and animal life in land habitats and water habitats, how living things find what they need to grow and survive in these habitats, and interrelationships between plants and animals.

## UNIT 5 Environments for Living Things

© Houghton Mifflin Harcourt Publishing Company • Image Credits: ©Paul Bradbury/OJO Images/Getty Images

# Lesson 1
# Plant Needs

Let's plant!

What do you notice about the sunflowers in the open field?

What do you wonder about the sunflowers in the open field?

## Can You Explain It?

Why can these sunflowers grow here?

_____

_____

_____

_____

# Explore Sunlight and Water

Gardening is an activity that is often done in spring and summer. People buy seeds to grow all types of plants, such as flowers and vegetables. Most plants get nutrients from soil. A **nutrient** is anything that living things need as food.

Ask a question about whether plants need sunlight and water to grow.

## Materials Checklist

☐ several plants of the same type
☐ measuring cup
☐ water

HMMM

### Step 1

Observe the plants. Record what you observe.

### Step 2

With the group, make a plan to find out whether plants need sunlight or water.

Why is it important to follow the order of the steps in your plan?

## Step 3

Follow your plan. Record your observations for your group every two to three days.

| | Sunlight | Water |
|---|---|---|
| 1 | | |
| 2 | | |
| 3 | | |
| 4 | | |

## Step 4

Talk with a classmate to complete the other half of the table. What causes the plants to grow differently?

_____

_____

_____

Make a **claim** about whether plants need sunlight and water to grow.

_____

_____

_____

What is your **evidence**? Talk with a partner about your **reasoning**.

I explored _____

_____

_____

How does this help me explain why sunflowers grow where they do?

_____

_____

_____

# Explore Space for Plants

Look at the plants growing close together. Each plant has roots that grow in the soil. Roots take in water and nutrients. They also hold a plant in place.

Ask a question about whether plants need space to grow.

_____

_____

_____

## Materials Checklist

☐ pictures of plants

### Step 1

Observe the pictures.
Talk with a small group.

### Step 2

Draw how plants look with
different amounts of space. Label the plants.

### Step 3

What was the effect of growing plants too
close to each other? Talk with a partner.

Make a **claim** about whether plants need space to grow.

_____

_____

_____

What is your **evidence**? Talk with a partner about your **reasoning**.

## Making Sense

I explored _____

_____

_____

How does this help me explain why sunflowers grow where they do?

_____

_____

# Lesson Check

## Can You Explain It?

Why can sunflowers grow here? Be sure to describe all the things that plants need to live and grow.

_____

_____

_____

_____

# Self Check

1. What do plants need to grow? Circle all correct answers.

2. Tyler and his family go away for two weeks. No one waters his plant while they are gone. What will the plant look like when they get home?

**3.** What would happen to this plant if it stopped getting sunlight and water?

_____

_____

_____

**4.** Jen observes that only one of the plants in her pot is bright green. All the other plants have droopy, yellow leaves. What is causing her plants to look this way?

_____

_____

_____

_____

# Plants Depend on Animals

Let's help plants!

What do you notice about the bee and the chipmunk?

What do you wonder about the bee and the chipmunk?

## Can You Explain It?

How do animals help plants?

_____

_____

_____

_____

# Engineer It
## Spread Seeds

wow!

Plants have seeds that can grow into new plants. These seeds need sunlight, water, air, and space. Because plants cannot move, they depend on animals to move seeds from place to place. Think about how the body parts of animals are shaped to move seeds.

Ask a question about how animals move seeds.

_____

_____

## Materials Checklist

☐ animal covering materials

☐ burdock seeds

HOW?

## Explore

**Step 1**

Explore the materials. Talk with a partner about what you observe.

**Step 2**

Choose three materials. Predict which ones will pick up seeds. Then lightly drag each material across the seeds. Record your results.

| Material | Prediction | Test Results |
|---|---|---|
| | Yes  No | Yes  No |
| | Yes  No | Yes  No |
| | Yes  No | Yes  No |

**Step 3**

What are some properties of materials that pick up seeds? Talk with a partner.

## Make

### Step 4

Design a tool to help people move seeds. Draw a picture of your tool, and label each part.

### Step 5

Compare your tool with a partner's tool. Tell how you got an idea from observing an animal or seeds.

 Tell how working with a partner helps you get ideas about how animals move seeds.

Make a **claim** about how animals move seeds.

_____

_____

What is your **evidence**? Talk with a partner about your **reasoning**.

## Making Sense ■ □

I explored _____

_____

_____

How does this help me explain how animals help plants?

_____

_____

_____

© Houghton Mifflin Harcourt Publishing Company

# Model Moving Pollen

**Pollen** is a light, sticky powder that flowers need to make seeds. Animals such as bees and ladybugs help move pollen as they feed on nectar deep within the flower. Think about how the body parts of animals are shaped to move pollen.

Ask a question about how animals move pollen.

## Materials Checklist

☐ 3 colors of chalk powder ☐ 3 cotton balls

☐ 3 small cups ☐ cotton swabs ☐ water

### Step 1

NEAT!

Place each powder in a different cup with a cotton ball. Dip a cotton swab in water. Roll it over each cotton ball. Record what you observe.

### Step 2

Repeat two more times. Compare your results with a partner.

### Step 3

What parts of an animal can help move pollen from plant to plant?

Make a **claim** about how animals
move pollen.

_____

_____

_____

What is your **evidence**? Talk with a
partner about your **reasoning**.

## Making Sense

I explored _____

_____

How does this help me explain how animals
help plants?

_____

_____

_____

# Lesson Check

## Can You Explain It?

How do animals help plants? Be sure to explain how the parts of animals help plants move seeds or pollen.

_____

_____

_____

_____

_____

# Self Check

1. What causes a bee to move pollen?

   Ⓐ The pollen is light and sticky.

   Ⓑ The pollen has structures like wings.

   Ⓒ The pollen has hooks that catch onto the bee.

2. What can you find out from a model of a seed?

   Ⓐ the shape of the seed

   Ⓑ the size of the seed

   Ⓒ the structure of the seed

3. Explain how this type of seed can be moved from place to place.

_____

_____

_____

_____

_____

_____

4. A farmer sees that his strawberry crop is not as large as it was last year. He reads in the newspaper that there are fewer bees in the area. What conclusion can you draw about why his crop is smaller?

_____

_____

_____

_____

_____

_____

# Lesson 3
# Plants and Animals in Land Habitats

In a rain forest!

What do you notice about the iguana and the zebra plant?

What do you wonder about the iguana and the zebra plant?

## Can You Explain It?

Why can an iguana and a zebra plant live in a rain forest and not in a desert?

_____

_____

_____

_____

# Model a Plant

In a forest, some trees are tall. They get a lot of sunlight. Other plants grow in the shady areas low to the ground. Cacti live in dry, hot deserts. They do not need a lot of water to grow. Other plants grow in rain forests and savannas.

Ask a question about why different plants grow in different places.

## Materials Checklist

☐ nonfiction books ☐ craft materials

☐ a computer

COOL!

## Step 1

Use nonfiction books or a computer to find out about different plants. Where do they grow? Why do they grow there?

## Step 2

Draw one plant you found out about, and show a place where it grows.

## Step 3

Use craft materials to make a model of the plant and where it grows. Compare your model with your classmate's models.

## Step 4

Think about all the models your classmates shared. What pattern do you observe?

Make a **claim** about why different plants grow in different places.

_____

_____

What is your **evidence**? Talk with a partner about your **reasoning**.

## Making Sense ▇ ☐

I explored _____

_____

How does this help me explain why an iguana and a zebra plant live in a rain forest and not in a desert?

_____

_____

_____

# Model an Animal

African elephants live in a savanna. Sloths live in a rain forest. These animals live in different habitats. A **habitat** is a place where a living thing can get the food, water, and shelter it needs to live and grow. Some habitats can be found in trees or in tall grasses.

Ask a question about why different animals live in different places.

_____

_____

_____

## Materials Checklist

☐ nonfiction books ☐ a computer

☐ craft materials ☐ shoebox

NEAT!

### Step 1

Use nonfiction books or a computer to find out about different types of animals. Where do they live? Why do they live there?

### Step 2

Draw the animal you found out about. Include its habitat in your picture. Tell about where your animal lives.

## Step 3

Use craft materials to make a model of the animal and the place where it lives. Compare your model with your classmate's models.

 How can you show respect to your classmates when they are sharing their models?

## Step 4

Think about all the models your classmates shared. What could happen if an animal were moved to a different place with a different habitat?

_____

_____

_____

Make a **claim** about why different animals live in different places.

_____

_____

What is your **evidence**? Talk with a partner about your **reasoning**.

## Making Sense

I explored _____

_____

_____

How does this help me explain why an iguana and a zebra plant live in a rain forest and not in a desert?

_____

_____

_____

# Lesson Check

## Can You Explain It?

Why can an iguana and a zebra plant live in a rain forest and not in a desert? Be sure to compare the features of a rain forest and a desert.

_____

_____

_____

_____

_____

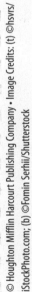

# Self Check

1. These animals live on the rain forest floor. Which patterns explain why they live there? Choose all correct answers.

    Ⓐ They have claws for climbing trees.

    Ⓑ They do well in a wet habitat.

    Ⓒ They can find the food they need in this habitat.

2. A zebra lives in a savanna. How does it get what it needs there? Choose all correct answers.

    Ⓐ It can find the food it needs.

    Ⓑ It can get the water it needs.

    Ⓒ It can find the shelter it needs.

**3.** This elephant lives in a savanna. Could it live in a forest? Explain why or why not.

_____

_____

_____

**4.** Amy makes a model of a cactus. Tarek makes a model of a desert tortoise. Both these living things live in a desert. What pattern can the children observe?

_____

_____

_____

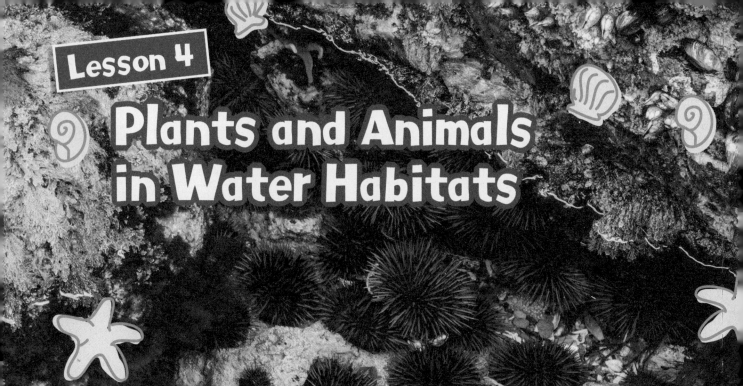

# Lesson 4
# Plants and Animals in Water Habitats

Salty or fresh?

What do you notice about the sea urchin and the catfish?

What do you wonder about the sea urchin and the catfish?

## Can You Explain It?

Why does a sea urchin live in a different place than a catfish?

_____

_____

_____

_____

# Compare Water Habitats

Ponds and river deltas are different places that have different habitats within them. A **habitat** is the place where a living thing can get the food, water, and shelter it needs to live and grow. Water habitats are under the water or near the water's edge.

Ask a question about why different plants and animals are found in different water habitats.

_____

_____

## Materials Checklist

☐ pictures of animals and plants
in water habitats

### Step 1

Observe the pictures. Talk with
a partner about the living things
found in each water habitat.
Think about why they live there.

### Step 2

Choose two water habitats. Draw the living
things in each one. Label your drawings.
Compare with your partner.

What might happen if a living thing from one habitat were moved to a different habitat?

Make a **claim** about why different living things are found in different water habitats.

_____

_____

What is your **evidence**? Talk with a partner about your **reasoning**.

## Making Sense ■☐

I explored _____

_____

How does this help me explain why a sea urchin lives in a different place than a catfish?

_____

_____

_____

# Hands On!

# Model a Water Habitat

This aquarium has salty water. Some aquariums have fresh water, which is water that is not salty. Plants and animals that live in saltwater aquariums cannot live in freshwater aquariums.

Ask a question about living things in an aquarium.

_____

_____

## Materials Checklist

☐ a small tank   ☐ water   ☐ aquarium soil   ☐ snails

☐ safety goggles   ☐ gloves   ☐ local freshwater plants

## Step 1

Observe the materials. With a partner, draw a plan to set up a freshwater habitat. Think about the type of water your habitat will need.

SWEET!

 Why is it important to finish the task before starting another?

## Step 2

Follow your plan. Build your model. Be sure to include all the materials your teacher gave you.

## Step 3

Record what you observe. Compare your observations with others.

| Day 1 | Day 2 | Day 3 | Day 4 |
| --- | --- | --- | --- |
| | | | |

## Step 4

Think about all the models your classmates made. What pattern did you observe?

Make a **claim** about living things in an aquarium.

_____

_____

What is your **evidence**? Talk with a partner about your **reasoning**.

## Making Sense

I explored _____

_____

How does this help me explain why a sea urchin lives in a different place than a catfish?

_____

_____

_____

# Lesson Check

## Can You Explain It?

Why does a sea urchin live in a different place than a catfish? Be sure to explain the differences between where a sea urchin lives and where a catfish lives.

_____

_____

_____

_____

_____

# Self Check

1. This plant lives in a small body of fresh water. The water is still so it doesn't move very much. Where does the plant live?

   Ⓐ in a pond

   Ⓑ in a river

   Ⓒ in an ocean

2. Melissa and Elizabeth are comparing water habitats. Elizabeth thinks that a fish from the ocean could live in a lake. Explain why or why not.

_____

_____

_____

_____

_____

_____

**3.** This alligator lives in a river. Could it live in the ocean? Explain why or why not.

_____

_____

_____

_____

_____

_____

_____

_____

**4.** Different water habitats have different living things. What is one thing that all habitats have in common?

ⓐ All habitats are large in size.

ⓑ All habitats have fresh water.

ⓒ All habitats have the food and water that living things need.

# Unit Review

**1.** What can cause a plant's leaves to be yellow and droopy? Choose all correct answers.

   Ⓐ not enough sunlight

   Ⓑ not enough water

   Ⓒ not enough wind

**2.** Sammy plants some flowers in the garden. He puts them very close together. What may happen to the flowers?

_____

_____

**3.** Sadie's plant does not look healthy. What does it need?

   Ⓐ soil

   Ⓑ shelter

   Ⓒ water

4. Observe the deer in the forest. Why does the deer live there?

_____

_____

_____

5. How do plants depend on animals? Choose all correct answers.

    Ⓐ They move plants from place to place.

    Ⓑ They move pollen so plants can make seeds.

    Ⓒ They move seeds so new plants can grow.

6. Look at these pond plants. What pattern do you observe?

    Ⓐ Both plants do not need sunlight.

    Ⓑ Both plants have leaves that are above the water.

    Ⓒ Both plants live underwater.

**7.** Observe the cypress trees in the river delta. A river delta has fresh water or a mix of fresh and salty water. Could cypress trees seeds grow near an ocean? Explain why or why not.

_____

_____

_____

_____

**8.** Susie observes burrs stuck to her socks. When she walks, the seeds fall off in different places. How can Susie build a tool to spread seeds?

_____

_____

_____

_____

# Interactive Glossary

This Interactive Glossary will help you learn how to spell and define a vocabulary term. The Glossary will give you the meaning of the term. It will also show you a picture to help you understand what the term means.

Where you see ▭ write your own words or draw your own picture to help you remember what the term means.

## Glossary Pronunciation Key

With every Glossary term, there is also a phonetic respelling. A phonetic respelling writes the word the way it sounds, which can help you pronounce new or unfamiliar words. Use this key to help you understand the respellings.

| Sound | As in | Phonetic Respelling |
|-------|-------|---------------------|
| a | bat | (BAT) |
| ah | lock | (LAHK) |
| air | rare | (RAIR) |
| ar | argue | (AR•gyoo) |
| aw | law | (LAW) |
| ay | face | (FAYS) |
| ch | chapel | (CHAP•uhl) |
| e | test | (TEST) |
|   | metric | (MEH•trik) |
| ee | eat | (EET) |
|   | feet | (FEET) |
|   | ski | (SKEE) |
| er | paper | (PAY•per) |
|   | fern | (FERN) |
| eye | idea | (eye•DEE•uh) |
| i | bit | (BIT) |
| ing | going | (GOH•ing) |
| k | card | (KARD) |
|   | kite | (KYT) |
| ngk | bank | (BANGK) |

| Sound | As in | Phonetic Respelling |
|-------|-------|---------------------|
| oh | over | (OH•ver) |
| oo | pool | (POOL) |
| ow | out | (OWT) |
| oy | foil | (FOYL) |
| s | cell | (SEL) |
|   | sit | (SIT) |
| sh | sheep | (SHEEP) |
| th | that | (THAT) |
|   | thin | (THIN) |
| u | pull | (PUL) |
| uh | medal | (MED•uhl) |
|   | talent | (TAL•uhnt) |
|   | pencil | (PEN•suhl) |
|   | onion | (UHN•yuhn) |
|   | playful | (PLAY•fuhl) |
|   | dull | (DUHL) |
| y | yes | (YES) |
|   | ripe | (RYP) |
| z | bags | (BAGZ) |
| zh | treasure | (TREZH•er) |

### compass rose (KUHM·puhs ROHZ)

A part of a map that shows directions north, south, east, and west. (p. 75)

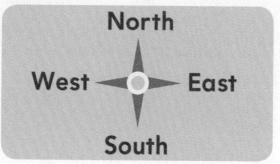

### design process (dih·ZYN PRAHS·es)

A set of steps that helps you find a solution. (p. xi)

### earthquake (ERTH·kwayk)

Causes a sudden shaking of the ground that makes land rise and fall. (p. 100)

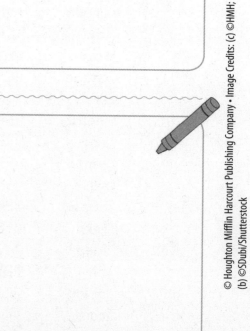

## engineer (en·juh·NEER)

A person who uses math and science to solve problems. (p. xi)

## erosion (uh·ROH·zhuhn)

The process of picking up and moving rocks, soil, or sand from one place to another. (p. 91)

## freeze (FREEZ)

A change in matter from liquid to solid. (p. 44)

### habitat (HAB·ih·tat)

A place where a living thing can get the food, water, air, and shelter needed to live. (pp. 159, 168)

### irreversible (ir·ih·VER·suh·buhl)

A change that cannot be undone. (p. 44)

### landform (LAND·fohrm)

A natural feature found on Earth's surface. (p. 72)

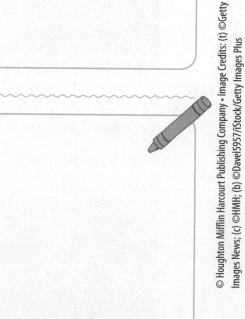

## landslide (LAND·slyd)

The sliding down of rocks and soil on or from a hill, mountain, or other slope. (p. 100)

**M**

## map key (MAP KEE)

A part of a map that shows what the colors and symbols mean. (p. 75)

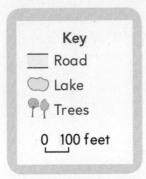

## matter (MAT·er)

Anything that takes up space. (p. 20)

## melt (MELT)

A change in matter from solid to liquid. (p. 48)

## model (MAHD·L)

Something that shows what an object looks like or how it works. (p. 4)

## nutrient (NOO·tree·uhnt)

Anything that living things need as food. (p. 132)

### pollen (PAHL·uhn)

A light, sticky powder that flowers need to make seeds. (p. 148)

### property (PRAHP·er·tee)

One part of what something is like. (p. 20)

### reversible (rih·VER·suh·buhl)

A change that can be undone. (p.44)

**S**

### solution (suh·LOO·shuhn)
Something that fixes a problem. (p. xi)

**V**

### volcano (vahl·KAY·noh)
An opening in Earth's surface where lava, gases, and bits of rock erupt. (p. 103)

**W**

### weathering (WETH·er·ing)
A process that breaks rock into smaller pieces. (p. 91)

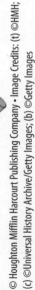

## windbreak (WIND·brayk)

Trees or shrubs planted to help block the wind. (p. 116)

# Index

© Houghton Mifflin Harcourt Publishing Company

# Index

COLOR Us!

Engineering robot

**Life Science robot**

— I am a scientist. —

KEEP going!

Physical Science robot

**Earth Science robot**

Science is FUN!